BEYOND ACCUSATION
THE VINDICATION
OF GOD'S CHARACTER

*A Devotional Journey Through the Great
Controversy and The Heart of God*

MICHAEL A. REAHL

DEDICATION

To those who have ever questioned why God allows pain, struggle, or silence, this is for you.

To the soldier who has seen too much, the believer who feels unheard, the pastor who wonders if God is still good, and the skeptic who can't see love through the world's darkness, this book is dedicated to you.

This journey is for every heart that has whispered, "Why, Lord?"

May these pages remind you that even when heaven seems quiet, God's love is speaking louder than the accusation.

TABLE OF CONTENTS

PREFACE

My previously published Devotional, 'Commissioned', reminds believers that the call to serve God isn't limited to pulpits or church pews; it reaches into every corner of daily life. Whether we wear a uniform, a badge, a stethoscope, or simply a willing heart, we are already standing in our mission field.

This new book, *Beyond Accusation*, grows from the same soil; but its roots reach deeper into the story behind every act of faith.

Why does God allow pain? Why do good people suffer? Why does evil seem to win while heaven watches?

I've wrestled with those questions in hospital hallways, on lonely patrols, and in quiet moments when prayers felt unanswered. Through those seasons, I came to see that life's hardest questions are not only about human suffering; they are about God's **character**.

From the very beginning, Satan accused God of being unjust, unloving, and unfair. Every act of rebellion, every moment of doubt, was built on that lie. The story of Scripture, from Eden to Calvary to the final restoration in Revelation, is God's patient answer to that accusation. The great controversy between good and evil is not just about us; it's about who God really is.

In these pages, I invite you to journey through that story, not as a theologian dissecting ideas, but as a fellow traveler learning what it means to trust the heart of God when everything else falls apart. We will explore how the cross, the law, judgment, and even suffering all point to one truth: God is love, and love always defends itself by revealing, not forcing.

This is not a book of arguments; it's a testimony of discovery. My hope is that as you read, you will see that the questions of the universe are answered not by explanations but by a Person. The God who stood accused chose to step into the courtroom of human pain and prove His love through a cross.

May this journey strengthen your faith, comfort your heart, and remind you that God's character does not need to be questioned, only to be seen.

"The Lord is righteous in all His ways and kind in all His works." *(Psalm 145:17, ESV)*

Michael A. Reahl

NOTE TO THE READER

This book is written to encourage every believer, regardless of role, background, or title, to live as a daily witness of God's character. The story of redemption is not a distant theory; it is the living reality of God's love working in human lives. Each chapter invites you to see your faith within the broader story of the Great Controversy: a conflict not merely between good and evil, but between truth and deception about who God really is.

Whether you serve in a church, a classroom, a home, or a mission field, your life becomes part of the evidence that vindicates God's name. Evangelism is not confined to pulpits or programs; it is the quiet, steady work of a heart surrendered to love and truth. May these pages deepen your faith, renew your trust in Scripture, and inspire you to live commissioned; with courage, integrity, and the peace of knowing that God's character is revealed through you.

AUTHOR'S NOTE ON SOURCES

Throughout this book, I have drawn primarily from the rich heritage of Adventist authors, theologians, and historical writings, voices that have faithfully upheld the truth about God's character and His plan of redemption. Insights from the *Seventh-day Adventist Encyclopedia*, the *Adventist Archives*, Ellen G. White's inspired writings, and scholarly works from *Andrews University Digital Commons* have all informed the ideas shared in these pages.

These sources have been prayerfully studied to ensure that every concept aligns with the central message of Scripture: the revelation of God's love through Jesus Christ and the final vindication of His character before the universe. Where other Christian writers are occasionally referenced, it is only to highlight shared biblical truths that harmonize with this great theme.

The purpose of every quotation and idea is singular; to lead the reader back to the Word of God, to a clearer vision of His heart, and to a deeper confidence in His goodness.

INTRODUCTION: THE STORY BEHIND THE CONFLICT

Before humanity's first breath, there was harmony in heaven. Every being lived in perfect freedom under a God of love. But that harmony was shattered when a created being, Lucifer, began to question God's character. He claimed that divine law was unfair, that obedience limited freedom, and that love was not enough to govern intelligent beings. (cf. Isa. 14:12–14; Ezek. 28:15–17; Rev. 12:7–9; Gen. 3:1–5).

That question, *'Is God truly good?'* , became the foundation of the Great Controversy, a conflict not over power but over trust. From that moment forward, God's character has been misunderstood, misrepresented, and maligned. Yet through every page of Scripture, through every act of mercy and justice, He has revealed who He truly is: a God whose government is built on love and whose greatest victory is not destruction, but redemption.

This book, *Beyond Accusation: The Vindication of God's Character*, is a journey through that story; a devotional exploration of how God's love responds to doubt, rebellion, and suffering. It is written for those who have ever questioned why pain exists, why faith is tested, or how God can still be good in a broken world.

The vindication of God's character is not a distant theological concept. It's the story of your life and mine. Every choice of faith, every act of kindness, every moment of endurance becomes part of heaven's testimony that God's way is just and His mercy endures forever.

1. Through these chapters, you will walk through four movements:

2. **The Accusation** – How rebellion began and God's character was questioned.
3. **The Defense of Love** – How the cross revealed truth and silenced deception.
4. **The Witnesses of His Character** – How believers today bear God's image through faithfulness.
5. **The Eternal Verdict** – How the universe will one day unite in the confession that *"just and true are Your ways, O Lord."*

This is not a book of arguments, but of evidence, the evidence of love. And in the end, every heart that trusts God becomes part of His vindication.

WRITING AND THEOLOGICAL FRAMEWORK

The message of *Beyond Accusation: The Vindication of God's Character* rests upon the foundation of the Great Controversy theme, a unifying lens through which Scripture, history, and experience reveal the justice, mercy, and love of God. The purpose of this framework is to explain both the theological grounding and the approach taken in writing this work.

THEOLOGICAL FOUNDATION

At its core, this book explores the Great Controversy as more than a cosmic narrative; it is the story of God's character on trial before the universe. The rebellion of Lucifer, the entrance of sin, the ministry of Christ, and the restoration of creation all revolve around one central question: *Is God truly good and just in all His ways?*

This perspective is deeply rooted in Scripture and reflected in the writings of Ellen G. White and Adventist theological scholarship. From the prophetic visions of Daniel and Revelation to the practical faith of Job and Paul, the Bible consistently portrays God's actions as transparent, righteous, and motivated by love. Christ's life and death stand as the ultimate revelation of divine character, the cross being the moment where justice and mercy met in perfect harmony.

In harmony with Adventist theology, this book views judgment not as condemnation but as vindication. Every act of divine judgment throughout history affirms God's fairness and exposes the destructiveness of sin. The investigative judgment, often misunderstood, is presented here not as a threat but as the ultimate expression of divine transparency, God allowing creation to see that His decisions are true and just.

WRITING APPROACH

The writing of *Beyond Accusation* intentionally blends devotional tone with theological depth. While it reflects academic rigor in its use of Scripture and Adventist scholarship, it is designed for readers from all walks of life, pastors, students, and believers seeking deeper faith. Each chapter moves from biblical exposition to spiritual reflection, inviting personal application rather than intellectual debate.

This balance of study and devotion follows a practical theology model, one that affirms that truth is best understood when lived. The aim is not to argue but to awaken to lead readers into a clearer understanding of God's love and their role in its revelation to the world.

Where appropriate, insights are drawn from respected Adventist scholars such as George R. Knight, Norman Gulley, Jiří Moskala, and Richard Davidson, as well as the inspired writings of Ellen G. White. Scripture remains the ultimate authority, interpreted through a Christ-centered, grace-filled lens consistent with the historic Seventh-day Adventist understanding of redemption and restoration.

PURPOSE AND APPLICATION

This work seeks to strengthen faith by helping readers see their lives as part of God's defense of truth. Every act of trust, compassion, and perseverance becomes a testimony in the ongoing story of the Great Controversy. The vindication of God's character is not merely a doctrinal concept; it is a lived reality, experienced in those who reflect His love in their homes, workplaces, and communities.

Beyond Accusation therefore serves not only as a theological study but as a devotional call, to live as daily witnesses that God's way is just, His grace sufficient, and His love unchanging.

PART I

THE ACCUSATION

CHAPTER 1:

THE BEGINNING OF REBELLION

- ▶ Lucifer's claim: "God is unjust and self-seeking."

- ▶ The first doubt in heaven.

- ▶ The nature of God's government:

- ▶ Love, freedom, and trust.

- ▶ The cost of free will.

Lucifer's Claim: "God is Unjust and Self-Seeking"

Before there was sin on earth, there was pride in heaven. The story of evil began not in darkness, but in light. In the presence of perfection, an angel named Lucifer, whose name means "light bearer," allowed a seed of pride to grow in his heart.

Ezekiel wrote, "You were blameless in your ways from the day you were created, till unrighteousness was found in you" (Ezekiel 28:15, ESV). That unrighteousness was the first distortion of truth. Scripture reveals that Lucifer's fall began with pride, self-exaltation, and a desire to take the place of God (Isaiah 14:13–14; Ezekiel 28:17). This spirit of rebellion led him to challenge the goodness and fairness of God's character. From Eden to Job to Revelation, Satan consistently questions God's motives, suggesting that His commands restrict freedom (Genesis 3:1–5), that His blessings manipulate obedience (Job 1:9–11), and that His government is unjust (Revelation 12:10).

While the Bible does not record a single speech where Lucifer lays out these accusations at once, the pattern of his words and actions throughout Scripture shows a consistent theme: he casts doubt on God's justice, God's law, and God's love. These accusations ignited the conflict that Scripture unfolds across its pages which was a controversy over whether God can be trusted and whether His way truly leads to life.

The First Doubt in Heaven

It's almost impossible to imagine doubt existing in a perfect world. Yet that's exactly where it began. Lucifer, surrounded by beauty and honor, began to question why only Christ should share the Creator's authority. He envied the Son's closeness to the Father and mistook equality of love for equality of position.

Isaiah captures his inner voice:

"I will ascend to heaven; I will set my throne on high... I will make my-self like the Most High." (Isaiah 14:13–14, ESV)

He wanted to be like God, but not in character; in power. Pride, comparison, and suspicion began to erode the trust that held heaven together. Lucifer whispered his questions among the angels, and the first seeds of doubt took root.

The tragedy of sin began not with disobedience but with disbelief: a failure to trust the heart of God.

The Nature of God's Government: Love, Freedom, and Trust

God's government is built on love, and love can never be forced. Every being in the universe serves God not because they must, but because they *want* to. That freedom is the greatest gift, and the greatest risk God ever gave.

Lucifer's rebellion was a test of that freedom. He claimed that divine law was unnecessary and restrictive, that love should be free from obedience. Yet love without obedience ceases to be love at all. It becomes selfishness disguised as liberty.

Revelation describes the result: "Now war arose in heaven, Michael and his angels fighting against the dragon" (Revelation 12:7, ESV). This was no physical war; it was a war of truth versus deception, trust versus accusation. The controversy that began in heaven was about God's character, not His strength.

Even as rebellion spread, God remained patient. He allowed Lucifer the freedom to reveal his true motives so that the entire universe could see the difference between self-exaltation and divine love.

The Cost of Free Will

When we speak of free will, we often think of choice as a privilege. But for God, it was a sacrifice. He knew that creating beings with freedom meant they could choose to reject Him. Yet He did it anyway because love without freedom isn't love, it's control.

When Lucifer fell, God did not destroy him. He allowed rebellion to run its course, knowing that only time would reveal the full consequence of sin. The universe needed to see that the path of self-rule leads only to pain and death.

That same freedom was later given to humanity. In Eden, Adam and Eve faced the same test of trust that Lucifer failed. The serpent repeated the same lie: "Did God actually say…?" (Genesis 3:1). Distrust entered the human heart, and the conflict that began in heaven took root on earth.

Yet even then, God's response was not destruction but redemption. His silence was not weakness; it was mercy. His patience was not indifference; it was love giving space for truth to be seen.

Scriptural Focus

- Ezekiel 28:12–17 – Describes Lucifer's perfection, pride, and fall.
- Isaiah 14:12–14 – Reveals his ambition to be "like the Most High."
- Revelation 12:7–9 – Portrays the heavenly conflict and Satan's expulsion.

Together, these passages reveal that the rebellion began with an accusation, not an act, a challenge to God's fairness, not His power.

Reflection

The same question that began in heaven still whispers through the world today: *'Can God be trusted?'* Every temptation, every doubt, every struggle of faith is a continuation of that first rebellion. Yet each time we choose to trust God's goodness instead of questioning His motives, we take our stand on the side of truth.

Love wins not through argument but through character. God's defense has always been Himself.

"The Lord is righteous in all His ways and kind in all His works." *(Psalm 145:17, ESV)*

CHAPTER 2:

THE CHARACTER ON TRIAL

- ▶ How sin questioned God's justice and truthfulness.

- ▶ The problem of theodicy; Is God fair?

- ▶ Early biblical narratives where God's motives were challenged.

How Sin Questioned God's Justice and Truthfulness

When Lucifer rebelled, he did more than defy God's authority; he questioned God's *character.* The foundation of heaven's harmony was trust, and that trust depended on the conviction that God was good. But when Lucifer's accusations spread, they introduced suspicion into a world that had never known doubt.

The essence of sin is not merely breaking God's law; it is believing that God Himself is not trustworthy. When Adam and Eve listened to the serpent in Eden, they were not only disobeying a command; they were agreeing with a claim. The enemy whispered the same lie he had once voiced in heaven: that God's rules are meant to restrict, not protect, that He is holding something back from His creation.

"Did God actually say…?" (Genesis 3:1, ESV).

That question has echoed through history. Every act of rebellion, every selfish choice, every injustice among humans is a reflection of that first disbelief in God's goodness.

Sin placed God on trial. The charge: that His justice is flawed, His motives suspect, and His ways unfair.

The Problem of Theodicy: Is God Fair?

The word *theodicy* means the defense of God's goodness in the presence of evil. Since the fall, humanity has struggled with this question: *'If God is good, why does He allow suffering?'*

From the book of Job to the cries of the prophets, the tension between justice and mercy has always tested faith. Job never learned the heavenly conversation that began his trials, yet he clung to one unshaken truth: "Though He slay me, I will hope in Him" (Job 13:15).

Behind Job's suffering was a larger purpose. Satan had claimed that humans only serve God for reward, that obedience was self-interest disguised as faith. God allowed Job's trial to answer that accusation, not to prove Job's strength, but to demonstrate His own faithfulness through a human life.

The book of Job reveals that the real courtroom is not on earth but in heaven. The question is not simply, "Why do people suffer?" but "Can God be trusted even when His ways are not understood?"

Early Biblical Narratives Where God's Motives Were Challenged

From the beginning, Satan's strategy has been to twist God's motives and misrepresent His character.

- In Eden (Genesis 3), he accused God of withholding knowledge, convincing humanity that sin would bring enlightenment.
- In Cain's jealousy (Genesis 4), he planted the idea that God's favor was partial, stirring anger and resentment.
- In the days before the Flood (Genesis 6), humanity believed it could define good and evil apart from God, until corruption filled the earth.

Each story reveals the same underlying deception: that humans can live apart from God and still find meaning and happiness. But every generation that followed proved the opposite, that life apart from God leads only to confusion, violence, and decay.

Sin's ultimate effect is to make people believe that God's justice is cruelty and His patience is weakness. Yet through every act of rebellion, God continues to show mercy, offering grace long before judgment.

"Righteousness and justice are the foundation of Your throne; stead-fast love and faithfulness go before You." *(Psalm 89:14, ESV)*

Even when His fairness is questioned, His love never changes.

The Character on Trial: Then and Now

The same accusation that began in heaven continues today. The world still asks: *'If God is love, why is there suffering?'* But the cross remains the answer that silences every charge. There, God did not explain His justice; He *demonstrated* it. In the suffering of His Son, He revealed both His hatred for sin and His compassion for sinners.

The universe has been watching this story unfold since the beginning. Every act of faith, every moment of surrender, every believer who holds fast to God in the dark contributes to the evidence that God's way is good.

In a world that doubts His fairness, the life of a faithful Christian becomes living testimony. We are the answer to the accusation, not by argument, but by reflection. When God's love is seen in us, His character stands vindicated once more.

Scriptural Focus

- Job 1–2 – Satan's challenge: 'Does Job serve God for nothing?'
- Genesis 3–6 – The progression of distrust from Eden to the Flood.
- Psalm 89:14 – God's government rests on righteousness and love.

Together, these passages show that the controversy has always centered on God's fairness.

Reflection

Every believer will face moments when God's silence feels like absence and His justice feels delayed. But faith is not built on explanations; it's built on trust. When we choose to believe that God is good even when life is not, we take our place in His defense.

God's reputation is not defended by power but by love, and love is revealed through endurance.

"The Lord is faithful in all His words and kind in all His works." (*Psalm 145:17*, ESV)

PART II

THE DEFENSE OF LOVE

CHAPTER 3:

THE CROSS AS GOD'S SELF-DISCLOSURE

- ▶ How Calvary settles the accusation.
- ▶ "Mercy and truth have met together." (Psalm 85:10)
- ▶ Christ as both Judge and Substitute.

How Calvary Settles the Accusation

From the moment rebellion began, God chose a path that no created mind could have imagined. He would not crush the accuser by force; He would answer him with love. Every false claim that God is selfish, unjust, or unmerciful, would be answered on one hill, on one cross, through one Man.

At Calvary, the universe saw what power could never reveal, the heart of God exposed. The Creator hung on the tree, taking the guilt of His creation. He bore every accusation without retaliation, every wound without bitterness. There, in the shadow of the cross, the lie was finally unmasked.

The universe had asked, *'What kind of God rules the world?'*

The cross replied, *'A God who would rather die for His enemies than live without them.'*

Sin claimed that God takes life to preserve His throne. The cross proved that God gives His life to preserve ours.

"Mercy and Truth Have Met Together" (Psalm 85:10)

The cross stands where divine mercy and unbending truth meet in perfect harmony. Justice demanded that sin be condemned; mercy demanded that sinners be forgiven. In Christ, both were fulfilled.

"Steadfast love and faithfulness meet; righteousness and peace kiss each other." (Psalm 85:10, ESV)

At Calvary, truth was not ignored; it was satisfied. The law that Lucifer called unfair was honored to its fullest measure. God did not change His standard to save humanity; He met His own standard by giving

Himself.

This is the beauty of the gospel: the Judge became the condemned, and the guilty were offered freedom. In one act, God proved that love is never at war with justice. The cross did not soften the law; it revealed the law's truest purpose, to show the depth of God's love and the seriousness of sin.

Christ as Both Judge and Substitute

When Jesus stood before Pilate, the irony of eternity unfolded. The Creator was judged by His creation. Yet unseen to the crowd, He was also their true Judge and their Substitute. Scripture says that "the Father judges no one, but has given all judgment to the Son" (John 5:22), and again that God "will judge the world in righteousness by a man whom He has appointed" (Acts 17:31). The One standing in silence before human authority was the very One to whom all authority had been given in heaven and on earth.

Isaiah had already declared it: "He was pierced for our transgressions; He was crushed for our iniquities" (Isaiah 53:5, ESV). At the cross, the Judge took the place of the guilty so that justice would be upheld and mercy extended. And because He is the "Son of Man" (John 5:27), fully God yet fully human, His judgment carries both divine righteousness and perfect understanding of the human condition.

In that moment, God's character was fully revealed. Heaven's government, once accused of cruelty, was shown to be built on self-sacrifice. The cross answered the question that began in heaven: Can God be trusted? Every drop of blood said, "Yes."

The Revelation of Divine Love

The Great Controversy will end not with argument but with revelation. Calvary remains the evidence that cannot be refuted. No angel, no demon, no skeptic can deny the testimony of a God who dies for the undeserving.

The cross is not only history; it is the present language of God's love to every generation. When we look to it, our questions find rest. We see that the Almighty is not distant but deeply personal, that His justice is never detached from compassion.

"For God so loved the world, that He gave His only Son, that whoever believes in Him should not perish but have eternal life." (John 3:16, ESV)

Scriptural Focus

- John 3:16–17 – God's love revealed through the gift of His Son.
- Romans 5:6–8 – "While we were still sinners, Christ died for us."
- Isaiah 53:4–6 – The prophecy of the suffering Servant who bears our guilt.

These texts reveal that the cross is God's ultimate self-disclosure, proof that love is not a theory but an act.

Reflection

The cross did not change God's heart toward us; it revealed what was there all along. Every time we forgive, serve, or love when it costs us something, we reflect that same character.

The Great Controversy continues, but the verdict was already written in crimson. God's throne stands secure because His love has been tested and found true.

"Greater love has no one than this, that someone lay down his life for his friends." (John 15:13, ESV)

CHAPTER 4:

LAW AND GRACE: HARMONY, NOT OPPOSITION

- ▶ The law as the transcript of God's character.
- ▶ Why grace doesn't cancel obedience.
- ▶ Paul's writings and the vindication of righteousness.
- ▶ Obedience as evidence, not currency.

The Law as the Transcript of God's Character

Every kingdom is known by its law, and the kingdom of heaven is no different. But unlike human governments that enforce through fear, God's law reveals His heart. It is not a list of restrictions; it is a portrait of His love.

When Lucifer rebelled, he attacked the law because he wanted to attack the Lawgiver. If the law could be shown as harsh or unnecessary, then God Himself could be portrayed as untrustworthy. Yet Scripture says, "The law of the Lord is perfect, reviving the soul" (Psalm 19:7, ESV).

The Ten Commandments are not arbitrary demands; they are reflections of God's character: truth, purity, justice, and mercy written in moral form. To disregard the law is to deny the very nature of God. To honor it is to mirror His holiness.

The law exposes what sin hides. It is not an enemy to grace but its foundation. Without the law, grace would have nothing to forgive, and love would have no standard by which to shine.

Why Grace Doesn't Cancel Obedience

One of Satan's most successful deceptions has been convincing people that grace removes the need for obedience. But the cross did not erase God's law; it confirmed it.

Jesus said, "If you love Me, you will keep My commandments" (John 14:15, ESV). Love doesn't replace obedience; it empowers it. Grace does not give permission to sin; it gives power to overcome it.

The same Spirit that convicts us of sin also enables us to live righteously. Paul declared, "Do we then overthrow the law by this faith? By no means! On the contrary, we uphold the law" (Romans 3:31, ESV).

Grace is not the cancellation of law but the revelation of love stronger than guilt. It turns duty into desire and command into calling.

Paul's Writings and the Vindication of Righteousness

Paul, often misunderstood as the apostle who opposed the law, was in truth its greatest defender. He saw clearly that the law could not save, but it could reveal the One who does. "The law is holy, and the commandment is holy and righteous and good" (Romans 7:12, ESV).

Through faith in Christ, the believer experiences the harmony that the Great Controversy had broken; the harmony between justice and mercy, obedience and grace. In Romans 8, Paul described this victory: "The righteous requirement of the law might be fulfilled in us, who walk not according to the flesh but according to the Spirit" (Romans 8:4, ESV).

The gospel doesn't remove righteousness; it restores it. It brings humanity back into alignment with the moral order of heaven. In doing so, it vindicates God's claim that His law is perfect, not oppressive.

When grace produces obedience, the lie of Satan is exposed. The universe sees that God's commands are not burdensome but liberating, because they reflect the very freedom of love.

Obedience as Evidence, Not Currency

Obedience has never been the price of salvation; it is the proof of transformation. The redeemed do not keep God's law to earn His favor; they keep it because they have already received His love.

To obey is not to buy salvation but to bear witness. Every act of faithfulness says to the watching universe that God's Spirit can indeed write His law on human hearts.

"For this is the covenant that I will make ... I will put My laws on their hearts, and write them on their minds." (Hebrews 10:16, ESV)

When believers live in obedience through grace, they become living testimonies of what heaven claimed all along, that God's law is good, that His way is possible, and that His love is stronger than sin.

Scriptural Focus

- Romans 3:31 – Faith upholds, not abolishes, the law.
- Romans 7:12 – The law is holy and good.
- Romans 8:1–4 – The Spirit fulfills righteousness within us.
- Galatians 2:20 – "I have been crucified with Christ…" life through grace.
- John 14:15 – Love and obedience united.

These passages show that law and grace are not rivals but partners in redemption.

Reflection

The cross proves that God's grace does not weaken His law; it magnifies it. Grace doesn't lower the standard; it lifts the sinner. Obedience becomes joy because it flows from a heart that has seen Calvary.

When we live in that balance, law honored, grace received, we reflect the harmony of heaven itself. The Great Controversy finds its answer not in words but in lives transformed by both.

"For the grace of God has appeared, bringing salvation for all people, training us to renounce ungodliness and to live self-controlled, upright, and godly lives." (Titus 2:11–12, ESV)

CHAPTER 5:

JUDGMENT AS VINDICATION, NOT CONDEMNATION

- ► The misunderstood purpose of judgment.

- ► "The books were opened." (Daniel 7:10)

- ► Judgment as heaven's declaration of fairness.

- ► The saints affirming God's justice.

The Misunderstood Purpose of Judgment

Few subjects are as feared or misunderstood as the judgment of God. To many, it sounds like condemnation, a divine courtroom where guilt outweighs mercy. Yet in Scripture, judgment is portrayed not as a weapon against humanity but as *a defense of God's character and His people.*

In Daniel's vision, he saw a scene unlike any earthly trial:

"The court sat in judgment, and the books were opened." (Daniel 7:10, ESV)

This was not a judgment to discover truth, God already knows all things, but to *reveal* truth to the universe. The judgment scene is God's way of demonstrating that His dealings with humanity have always been fair, merciful, and transparent.

In this courtroom, God is not the accuser; He is the Advocate. The accuser is Satan; the same one who has misrepresented God from the beginning. The purpose of judgment is to expose that lie and to show that salvation is not arbitrary but just.

"The Books Were Opened"

The phrase "the books were opened" symbolizes God's complete transparency. Nothing is hidden in His government. The universe is invited to see how He has dealt with every life, every choice, every tear.

This imagery reassures believers that God's justice is never secretive or biased. Each record reveals not just sin, but mercy; not just failure, but redemption. The very act of opening the books demonstrates that God has nothing to hide.

For the redeemed, judgment is not something to fear but to anticipate. It is the moment when God declares before the universe that His grace was enough, His promises were true, and His people were faithful through His power.

"There is therefore now no condemnation for those who are in Christ Jesus." (Romans 8:1, ESV)

In judgment, God is not searching for reasons to condemn but presenting evidence to vindicate, both His people and Himself.

Judgment as Heaven's Declaration of Fairness

Throughout history, Satan has accused God of favoritism and inconsistency. He has claimed that divine justice cannot be both merciful and fair. But in judgment, every question is answered.

The cross proved that God's love could save; the judgment proves that God's salvation is just. These two realities, love and law, find perfect harmony in Christ's work.

Ecclesiastes declares, "God will bring every deed into judgment, with every secret thing, whether good or evil" (Ecclesiastes 12:14, ESV). This is not a threat; it's a promise that evil will not have the final word. No injustice will remain unaddressed. No act of faith will go unnoticed.

The judgment is heaven's public declaration that God's rule has been righteous all along.

The Saints Affirming God's Justice

In Revelation, John describes a moment when the redeemed stand with God and proclaim,

"Just and true are Your ways, O King of the nations!" (Revelation 15:3, ESV)

They do not fear judgment; they *agree* with it. Having experienced both mercy and discipline, forgiveness and faithfulness, they see clearly what sin tried to obscure: that God's justice is pure love in action.

The saints become witnesses, affirming before the universe that God's way is right. Their lives, once scarred by sin but restored by grace, become the living evidence that God's mercy does not compromise His righteousness.

When the great controversy finally closes, no one will question God's fairness again. Every heart will confess, "The Lord is righteous in all His works." (Psalm 145:17, ESV)

Scriptural Focus

- Daniel 7:9–10 – The judgment scene: "The books were opened."
- Revelation 14:6–7 – "Fear God and give Him glory, for the hour of His judgment has come: and worship Him…."
- Ecclesiastes 12:13–14 – Every deed brought into judgment by a just God.
- Romans 8:1 – No condemnation for those in Christ.

These passages reveal judgment as both revelation and vindication; a testimony that God's justice is perfect and His mercy complete.

Reflection

The purpose of judgment is not to reveal how sinful we are; it's to reveal how faithful God has been. Heaven's verdict will not expose the weakness of believers but the strength of divine grace.

When the books are opened, it will not be to shame the forgiven but to silence the accuser. God will be vindicated, and those who trusted Him will stand as living proof that His love was enough.

"The Lord is righteous in all His ways and kind in all His works." (Psalm 145:17, ESV)

PART III

THE WITNESSES OF HIS CHARACTER

CHAPTER 6:

THE VINDICATED LIFE: REFLECTING GOD IN THE BELIEVER

- ► The believer as living testimony.
- ► "We are a spectacle to the universe." (1 Corinthians 4:9)
- ► Sanctification as a cosmic witness.
- ► Modern reflections: faith, integrity, and mission.

The Believer as Living Testimony

The Great Controversy is not only fought in heaven or through history; it unfolds in the heart of every believer. Each day, unseen worlds watch as men and women choose between trust and doubt, obedience and rebellion, love and self. The controversy continues, not through angels or prophets, but through ordinary lives shaped by extraordinary grace.

The apostle Paul wrote, "You show that you are a letter from Christ… written not with ink but with the Spirit of the living God" (2 Corinthians 3:3, ESV). Every believer becomes a living testimony of who God is. When His character is reflected in human behavior, kindness, forgiveness, humility, the accusations of the enemy are answered once again.

The Christian life is not a performance to earn approval but a demonstration of what grace can do. The world may not read the Bible, but it reads our lives. What it sees in us will either confirm the lie that God's standards are impossible or reveal the truth that His Spirit transforms what sin has broken.

"We Are a Spectacle to the Universe" (1 Corinthians 4:9)

Paul described believers as being "a spectacle to the world, to angels, and to men." In other words, our faith is being observed, not for judgment, but for testimony. The way we respond to hardship, temptation, and adversity is part of a much larger story being told beyond human sight.

When we forgive those who wrong us, when we trust God's timing, when we choose honesty over advantage, we do more than live morally; we declare something about God's nature. Our lives become evidence that His grace truly restores.

Every act of faith, no matter how small, ripples through eternity. Heaven rejoices not over perfection, but over perseverance, the quiet, steadfast faith of those who keep believing when it would be easier to walk away.

Sanctification as a Cosmic Witness

Sanctification is often misunderstood as human effort to reach perfection, but Scripture presents it as divine partnership. It is not the believer trying harder; it is God revealing Himself through willing hearts.

"It is God who works in you, both to will and to work for His good pleasure." (Philippians 2:13, ESV)

Sanctification is the ongoing proof that the accusations of Satan are false. The enemy claims that God's law cannot be obeyed, that grace cannot truly change the human heart. But every transformed life, every victory over temptation, every act of selfless love says otherwise.

When God's Spirit produces His character in us, the Great Controversy shifts from theory to evidence. The same Spirit that empowered Christ now empowers His people to live as reflections of divine love.

Sanctification does not make us sinless; it makes us surrendered. And a surrendered life is the most powerful argument in favor of God's government.

Modern Reflections: Faith, Integrity, and Mission

In every age, God has raised up witnesses to reflect His character in their generation. Today, that calling rests on us. In our homes, workplaces, and communities, we carry the same mission: to show that God is good, trustworthy, and loving.

"Let your light shine before others, so that they may see your good works and give glory to your Father who is in heaven." (Matthew 5:16, ESV)

Faithful living in the modern world requires courage. It means holding integrity when compromise seems easier. It means showing compassion when the world is cold. It means living unashamed of grace in a culture that glorifies self.

Every believer, soldier, student, pastor, parent, is a missionary in the unseen conflict between truth and deception. When people see peace where they expected anger, joy where they expected bitterness, and forgiveness where they expected revenge, they are seeing the evidence that God's Spirit is still at work.

Scriptural Focus

- Matthew 5:16 – Let your light shine; glorify the Father through good works.
- 1 Corinthians 4:9 – Believers as a spectacle to the world and to angels.
- Romans 12:1–2 – Present your bodies as living sacrifices; be transformed.
- 1 John 2:6 – "Whoever says he abides in Him ought to walk in the same way."
- Philippians 2:13 – God works in us to will and to act according to His purpose.

Together, these verses reveal that sanctified living is not about earning God's approval; it's about proving His grace is real.

Reflection

Every generation produces witnesses, not the loudest or the most visible, but those whose quiet faith tells the truth about God when the world doubts Him most.

The life that reflects Christ becomes part of God's final argument: that His Spirit is stronger than sin, that His love is more powerful than hate, and that His character is still the hope of the world.

"We love because He first loved us." (1 John 4:19, ESV)

CHAPTER 7:

SUFFERING AND THE DEFENSE OF GOD'S NAME

- ▶ Job's story revisited: loyalty under fire.

- ▶ The silence of God as the test of faith.

- ▶ The martyrs and endurance as evidence.

- ▶ How trials reveal God's faithfulness through His people.

Scriptural focus: 2 Corinthians 4:7–10; Hebrews 11; Revelation 6:9–11.

Job's Story Revisited: Loyalty Under Fire

Long before theology was written in books, it was lived in the life of a man named Job. His story begins not on earth but in heaven, where a question was raised before the heavenly council: *Does Job fear God for nothing?*

Satan's challenge was not about Job's comfort; it was about God's character. He claimed that humanity's loyalty was bought with blessing, that obedience was a transaction and not love. If Job lost everything, Satan argued, his faith would collapse, and God's claim of transforming grace would be proven false.

When the trials came, Job's world fell apart, his family, his possessions, his health. Yet through pain and confusion, Job clung to one truth that silence could not erase: "Though He slay me, I will hope in Him" (Job 13:15, ESV).

Job's endurance was not proof of human strength but of divine faithfulness. In his suffering, the universe witnessed what Satan denied; a heart that loved God for who He is, not for what He gives.

The Silence of God as the Test of Faith

Perhaps the hardest part of suffering is not pain but the silence that follows it. When heaven seems quiet, when prayers echo back unanswered, doubt whispers the same question it asked in Eden: *Is God truly good?*

Yet silence does not mean absence. God's silence is often His trust; trust that His children know His heart well enough to walk by faith when they cannot see.[1]

Job did not receive explanations, but he received revelation. Out of the storm came the voice of God, not to defend Himself, but to remind Job that divine wisdom goes far beyond human understanding. Faith is not knowing all the answers; it is knowing the One who never changes.

"For we walk by faith, not by sight." (2 Corinthians 5:7, ESV)

Satan claimed that suffering would separate people from God; grace proved that suffering can draw them closer.

The Martyrs and Endurance as Evidence

Throughout history, millions have stood as living evidence of faith under fire. The early Christians who faced lions, the Reformers who faced flames, the missionaries who faced death in distant lands, all bore silent testimony that God's presence is enough.

Revelation 6 speaks of "the souls of those who had been slain for the word of God." They cry out not for revenge but for vindication, that truth might triumph, that justice might be seen.

Their endurance is not born of stubbornness but of love. They remind us that faith is strongest when it costs something. Every martyr's story is another answered accusation, that God's love can hold the human heart even when the world takes everything else.

"They have conquered him by the blood of the Lamb and by the word of their testimony."[2] (Revelation 12:11, ESV)

How Trials Reveal God's Faithfulness Through His People

Suffering does not prove God's absence, it reveals His nearness in ways

1 Ellen G. White, Education (Mountain View, CA: Pacific Press, 1903), 151–154.

2 Richard M. Davidson, "Revelation's Overcomers and Witness," JATS 24, no. 1 (2013): 87–92.

comfort never could. In hardship, God's people become reflections of His patience, mercy, and strength.

Paul wrote, "We are afflicted in every way, but not crushed; perplexed, but not driven to despair; persecuted, but not forsaken; struck down, but not destroyed" (2 Corinthians 4:8–9, ESV). The believer's endurance is not human determination; it is divine grace under pressure.

The world may see weakness, but heaven sees victory. Each trial faced with faith adds another line to the eternal testimony that God's love cannot be shaken.

When His children trust Him in pain, they give the universe a glimpse of Calvary again, the place where suffering did not defeat love but displayed it.

Scriptural Focus

- Job 1–2; 13:15 – Satan's accusation and Job's unwavering trust.
- 2 Corinthians 4:7–10 – Treasure in jars of clay; God's power through weakness.
- Hebrews 11:32–40 – Faith that endures despite loss.
- Revelation 6:9–11 – The martyrs cry for vindication.
- Revelation 12:11 – Victory through the Lamb and the word of testimony.

These texts show that suffering is not wasted; it becomes sacred evidence that faith and love can outlast pain.

Reflection

Suffering has never been God's weapon; it is often His witness. When believers endure hardship without losing hope, they echo the same truth that Job, the martyrs, and Christ Himself proclaimed: love is stronger than death.

The greatest defense of God's character is not a sermon or a system; it is a soul that still praises Him in the storm.

"My grace is sufficient for you, for My power is made perfect in weakness." (2 Corinthians 12:9, ESV)

CHAPTER 8:

THE FINAL CONFLICT

- ▶ The last deception and the call to loyalty.
- ▶ God's seal vs. the mark of the beast.
- ▶ Worship, allegiance, and truth under pressure.
- ▶ The closing of the Great Controversy.

The Last Deception and the Call to Loyalty

Every story in Scripture moves toward one final moment, the complete exposure of truth and deception. The Great Controversy that began with a lie in heaven will end with a verdict on earth. At the center of that conflict is a single question that has never changed: *Who is worthy of our worship?*

Revelation 13 describes a time when loyalty to God will again be tested. Human systems will demand allegiance, false worship will rise, and the pressure to conform will reach every nation. Yet even then, God's purpose remains the same, to reveal love through faithfulness.

This is not merely a test of endurance; it is a test of affection. The final conflict will separate those who serve God because they love Him from those who serve Him out of fear or convenience. Occupancy in the Kingdom of Heaven will not be determined by denomination but by devotion.

When the world bows to fear, God's people will stand in faith.

God's Seal vs. the Mark of the Beast

Throughout Scripture, seals represent ownership and authority. God's seal is placed on those who belong fully to Him; those who have surrendered heart and mind to His Spirit. Revelation 7:3 describes angels holding back the winds of destruction "until we have sealed the servants of our God on their foreheads."[3]

The mark of the beast, in contrast, symbolizes allegiance to a counterfeit authority; a system built on coercion instead of love. It is the final

---

3 Ellen G. White, The Great Controversy, 603–612 (chaps. "The Impending Conflict"; "The Final Warning").

expression of Lucifer's old claim that obedience to God is restrictive and that self-rule brings freedom.

Yet in the end, the mark is not about symbols or surface; it is about loyalty. The forehead represents conviction; the hand represents action. The conflict will not hinge on ritual but on relationship, who we trust, who we love, and whose character we reflect.

The seal of God is not earned by effort; it is received by surrender. Those who bear it have learned to rest in His righteousness rather than their own.

Worship, Allegiance, and Truth Under Pressure

At the height of the final crisis, worship becomes the dividing line. The issue will not be religion itself but *the nature of worship;* will it be compelled or chosen, fearful or faithful, false or true?

Revelation 14 depicts a people who refuse to compromise:

"Here is a call for the endurance of the saints, those who keep the commandments of God and their faith in Jesus." (Revelation 14:12, ESV)[4]

Their faithfulness under pressure testifies that God's grace can hold the human heart even in chaos. They keep God's commandments not to earn salvation but because they love the One who saved them. Their obedience is not resistance against the world but loyalty to heaven.

In a culture that worships power, they worship humility. In a time of deception, they cling to truth. And in a world that prizes compromise, they stand with courage.

Their endurance does not glorify human strength; it vindicates divine faithfulness.

------

4 Ángel Manuel Rodríguez, "Seal of God/Mark of the Beast: Theological Perspectives," BRI Research Paper (Silver Spring, MD: Biblical Research Institute, 2010), 4–9.

The Closing of the Great Controversy

When the conflict ends, no one will misunderstand God again. The universe will see that every act of judgment, every delay, every moment of mercy was driven by love. The controversy that began with accusation will close with adoration.

"Just and true are Your ways, O King of the nations!" (Revelation 15:3, ESV)

Every knee will bow, not from fear, but from conviction. Even those who once doubted will acknowledge that God was right, that His law was just, and that His patience was mercy.

Daniel 12 describes the end of this conflict: "At that time your people shall be delivered, everyone whose name shall be found written in the book." The war ends not with destruction but with deliverance. The redeemed will stand as eternal witnesses that love never failed.

The universe will forever echo the truth that has been proven by the cross, the church, and the faithful: God was never the accuser; He was the answer.

Scriptural Focus

- Revelation 13–15 – The final test of worship and the endurance of the saints.
- Daniel 12:1–3 – Deliverance of God's people and the promise of resurrection.
- Romans 14:11 – Every knee shall bow; every tongue confess God's righteousness.
- Revelation 15:3–4 – "Just and true are Your ways."

These texts show that the closing conflict is not about power but about trust, not about control but about love.

Reflection

The last battle will not be fought with weapons but with hearts. The world will divide between those who live by fear and those who live by faith. And when it is over, one truth will remain: God's love never fails, and His people never stand alone.

Your loyalty today is the preparation for that day. Every small act of faithfulness now is training for the final witness then.

"Be faithful unto death, and I will give you the crown of life." (Revelation 2:10, ESV)

PART IV

THE ETERNAL VERDICT

CHAPTER 9:

LOVE REIGNS SUPREME

- ▶ The restoration of universal harmony.

- ▶ All creation united under God's love.

- ▶ The end of rebellion; no more accusation.

- ▶ Eternity as the ongoing revelation of divine character.

The Restoration of Universal Harmony

When the Great Controversy ends, the story of sin will close forever. The rebellion that began in heaven and scarred the earth will have been answered fully and finally. The universe will stand in perfect harmony again, not because fear enforces obedience, but because love commands loyalty.

The final chapters of Revelation paint the picture of that restored creation:

"Then I saw a new heaven and a new earth, for the first heaven and the first earth had passed away." (Revelation 21:1, ESV)

The brokenness of time will give way to the beauty of eternity. Death will be no more, tears will be wiped away, and every trace of sin will be erased, not by force, but by love fulfilled. The cross will forever remain the center of remembrance, the eternal evidence that God's justice and mercy were one.

Harmony returns when every being freely acknowledges that God's way was right all along.

All Creation United Under God's Love

Sin divided; love reunites. Every rift caused by rebellion, between heaven and earth, God and humanity, will be healed in Christ. The same love that reached into a manger and stretched upon a cross will now fill the universe with light.

Paul foresaw this moment when he wrote, "In Christ, all things hold together" (Colossians 1:17, ESV). What sin shattered, grace restores. What pride corrupted, humility redeems.

Every creature, from the angels who never fell to the redeemed who once did, will live in perfect unity, their voices joined in one song:

"To Him who sits on the throne and to the Lamb be blessing and honor and glory and might forever and ever!" (Revelation 5:13, ESV)

There will be no more suspicion, no more fear, no more misunderstanding of God's motives. The accusation that began with Lucifer will be forgotten, not because it was erased from memory, but because its answer will be eternally visible in the Lamb.

The End of Rebellion: No More Accusation

Nahum wrote, "Affliction shall not rise up a second time" (Nahum 1:9, KJV). The Great Controversy will never happen again because its lesson will never fade. Every being in the universe will have seen the full outcome of sin, the misery it brought, the suffering it caused, and the cost it required.[5]

The scars in Christ's hands will remain as the universe's eternal testimony. They will remind creation of what love endured and what it conquered. These scars are not marks of defeat, but of victory, permanent evidence that God's character has been vindicated beyond all question.

The silence of accusation will not be enforced; it will be voluntary. The universe will have seen the truth, and the truth will have set it free.

"Every creature in heaven and on earth… saying, 'To Him who sits on the throne and to the Lamb be blessing and honor and glory and might forever and ever!'" (Revelation 5:13, ESV)

Eternity as the Ongoing Revelation of Divine Character

Heaven will not be static perfection; it will be endless discovery. The redeemed will spend eternity learning new depths of God's love, exploring wonders of His wisdom, and rejoicing in the beauty of His

5 George R. Knight, The Cosmic Conflict, 171–176.

presence. Every age will unfold new reasons to worship, new insights into His kindness.

Ellen White wrote, *"The cross of Christ will be the science and the song of the redeemed through all eternity."*[6] That statement captures eternity's heartbeat: worship that never grows old because love never stops revealing itself.

Even in perfection, God will continue to share Himself. Heaven will not be about escaping the world but about entering into the fullness of His world, where every life, every voice, and every heart reflects His character without distortion.

The great question, *Is God love?*, will echo no more, for the answer will be visible everywhere.

Scriptural Focus

- Revelation 21:1–7 – The new heaven and new earth; God dwelling with His people.
- Revelation 22:1–5 – The river of life and the throne of God and the Lamb.
- Isaiah 65:17–25 – Joy and peace in the restored creation.
- Nahum 1:9 – Sin and affliction shall never rise again.
- Colossians 1:17–20 – All things reconciled in Christ.

Together, these texts reveal that eternity will be more than reward, it will be restoration, communion, and unending revelation of divine love.

Reflection

When time ends and eternity begins, one truth will remain: love reigns. Every act of rebellion, every shadow of doubt, every wound of sin will be swallowed by the brilliance of God's goodness.

Heaven is <u>not</u> merely a place to live, it is the experience of knowing

6 Ellen G. White, The Great Controversy, 651 (chap. 42, "The Controversy Ended").

God without barrier, fear, or misunderstanding. The universe will finally rest because love has proven itself completely.

"The Lord will be king over all the earth. On that day the Lord will be one and His name one." (Zechariah 14:9, ESV)

CHAPTER 10:

THE GOD WHO WAS NEVER WRONG

- ▶ What vindication means for faith today.

- ▶ God's patience and our trust.

- ▶ Living as witnesses of His goodness.

- ▶ Leadership, integrity, and devotion in the light of eternity.

Scriptural focus: *Psalm 145:17; Romans 11:33; Philippians 2:13–15.*

What Vindication Means for Faith Today

The story of God's vindication is not just a cosmic drama; it's a personal calling. To know that God has been proven right before the universe gives every believer confidence to live with purpose and peace. The cross, the judgment, and the restoration all point to one reality: God has never been wrong.

Every act of love, every answered prayer, every redeemed life is a living reminder that His character stands unblemished. In a world that questions truth, mocks holiness, and doubts goodness, we can rest in the certainty that God's word and His ways have never failed.

Vindication is not only heaven's verdict; it is the believer's assurance. It means that our faith is not misplaced, our hope is not naive, and our trust is not in vain.

"The Lord is righteous in all His ways and kind in all His works." (Psalm 145:17, ESV)

When we stand on that truth, we live with the quiet courage of those who already know the ending.

God's Patience and Our Trust

From the first rebellion in heaven to the final restoration of earth, God's response to accusation has been consistent,patient love. He could have silenced rebellion instantly, but instead He chose to let truth unfold slowly so that no one could ever doubt His fairness again.

That same patience defines His work in us. Just as He allowed time to prove His justice to the universe, He allows time to shape His character in our lives. Sanctification is God's vindication written in the human heart, His Spirit proving, moment by moment, that His grace can transform what sin once ruled.[7]

We may not always understand His timing, but we can always trust His heart. What seems like delay is often preparation; what feels like silence is often the sound of patience.

"Oh, the depth of the riches and wisdom and knowledge of God! How unsearchable are His judgments and how inscrutable His ways!" (Romans 11:33, ESV)

Living as Witnesses of His Goodness

Every believer is a piece of evidence in the ongoing revelation of God's character. The way we love, forgive, and lead tells the world what we believe about Him. Our lives may be the only testimony some will ever read.

Paul reminded the Philippians, "Do all things without grumbling or disputing, that you may be blameless and innocent, children of God without blemish in the midst of a crooked and twisted generation, among whom you shine as lights in the world." (Philippians 2:14–15, ESV)

We shine not by perfection but by reflection, by letting the light of God's character radiate through ordinary acts of faithfulness. Every kind word, every patient response, every moment of integrity is a defense of divine love before a watching world.

The vindication of God's character continues every day through His people. When the world sees Christ in us, the ancient accusation loses its power once again.

Leadership, Integrity, and Devotion in the Light of Eternity

To lead is to reflect the heart of the One who serves. True leadership, spiritual, personal, or professional, mirrors the nature of God: humble,

---

7 Ellen G. White, Steps to Christ, 67–72 (chap. "Growing Up Into Christ").

just, and faithful. The higher the responsibility, the greater the opportunity to reveal His character.

Integrity is not about reputation but representation. When we act with honesty, humility, and compassion, we lead others toward the truth about who God is. Our devotion becomes a living sermon that preaches louder than words ever could.

"It is God who works in you, both to will and to work for His good pleasure." (Philippians 2:13, ESV)

Leadership in the light of eternity means living with the awareness that everything we do echoes in the cosmic courtroom.[8] Every decision is part of the testimony that God's way works, that His Spirit transforms, and that His name is worthy of trust.

When we live with that vision, we lead with purpose.

Scriptural Focus

- Psalm 145:17 – God's righteousness and kindness in all His works.
- Romans 11:33 – God's wisdom and unsearchable judgments.
- Philippians 2:13–15 – God working in His people to shine as lights.
- 2 Corinthians 5:20 – Believers as ambassadors for Christ.

These verses remind us that vindication is not only a past event or future reality; it is a present calling to live as daily witnesses of divine goodness.

Reflection

The story ends where it began, with God, and with love.

---

8 Ellen G. White, The Ministry of Healing (Mountain View, CA: Pacific Press, 1905), 470–478 (chap. "A Higher Experience").

Lucifer's accusation has been answered. The cross stands eternal. The redeemed stand vindicated, and God stands proven true.

But until the day we see Him face to face, the greatest testimony we can offer is trust. When we live with joy in hardship, with hope in uncertainty, and with faith in silence, we echo heaven's final verdict: *God was right all along.*

"To Him be glory forever. Amen." (Romans 11:36, ESV)

EPILOGUE – A LIFE BEYOND ACCUSATION

When the story of sin is finally over, there will be no more debates, no more accusations, and no more questions about who God is. The cross will still stand at the center of eternity as the evidence that ended every doubt. But for those who know Him now, the verdict is already clear; **God has always been love, and love has never failed.**

Every generation has been part of this story. The prophets proclaimed it, the apostles lived it, and the faithful have carried it through every age. Yet the story isn't finished until it is told through *our* lives. The Great Controversy may one day close in heaven, but its message continues on earth through believers who choose to reflect God's character in a world that still misunderstands Him.

We are called to live *beyond accusation,* to rise each day as quiet witnesses that truth still triumphs, that grace still redeems, and that love still changes hearts. Our words may falter, our strength may fade, but the God who was vindicated through a cross still reveals Himself through surrendered lives.

He doesn't ask us to defend Him with arguments, but to **display Him through faithfulness.**[9] Every act of forgiveness, every decision to trust, every prayer whispered in darkness becomes part of His defense. The same patience that carried Him through Calvary now works through His people to show the world what love really looks like.

Someday, every question will be answered. Every tear will make sense. Every act of faith will be remembered. And when the universe stands in silent awe before the throne, no one will speak of how strong the redeemed were; they will speak of how good God has always been.

9 Ellen G. White, Education, 17–18; 225–227.

Until that day, we live to tell the truth that sets us free.

We live to show that the God who was once accused is forever adored. We live because His name has already been cleared and His love is still the greatest story ever told.

"Now to Him who is able to keep you from stumbling and to present you blameless before the presence of His glory with great joy, to the only God, our Savior, through Jesus Christ our Lord, be glory, majesty, dominion, and authority, before all time and now and forever. Amen." *(Jude 24–25, ESV)*

ABOUT THE AUTHOR

Michael A. Reahl lives and serves in Alaska, where faith and service meet in everyday life. A U.S. Army National Guard Infantry Officer and Police Officer, Michael has built his ministry on the front lines of both public safety and spiritual leadership. His calling is simple yet profound: to live the gospel where life happens and to help others see that every field of duty is a mission field.

He holds a Master of Theological Studies and a Bachelor of Science in Public Health, combining biblical knowledge with real-world experience in leadership, wellness, and community care. He has also served as a lifeguard trainer, medical instructor, and educator in prehospital emergency medicine, teaching courses such as CPR, ACLS, PALS, NRP, ITLS, and PHTLS.

Michael's background in both the military and medical fields has shaped his deep conviction that evangelism is not confined to pulpits or sanctuaries. Whether leading a team, training first responders, or standing watch in uniform, he sees every act of service as a reflection of God's presence.

Beyond his professional and ministry roles, Michael has participated in mission work around the world, including Ghana, Mexico, Cambodia, Mongolia, and other nations, where he has witnessed the power of the gospel to heal, unify, and transform. He also served as a colporteur, sharing Christian literature door to door and learning firsthand that the most meaningful ministry often begins with a simple conversation.

Through his writing and teaching, Michael seeks to awaken believers to their personal calling to evangelism. His passion is to remind readers that ministry belongs to every Christian, regardless of title or training, that faith must be lived as well as spoken.

In *Beyond Accusation: The Vindication of God's Character*, Michael invites readers into a deeper understanding of God's love and justice. Through Scripture, reflection, and practical faith, he reminds us that the truest defense of God is not in words, but in lives transformed by grace.

59

BIBLIOGRAPHY

The following works provided theological insight, spiritual direction, and historical context for *Beyond Accusation: The Vindication of God's Character.*

While this volume is written as a devotional exploration of the Great Controversy theme, it draws strength from the writings, research, and testimonies that have helped define Adventist theology and Christian thought throughout history.

Primary Sources and References

The Holy Bible – English Standard Version (ESV).

Andrews, John N. *The Sanctuary and the Twenty-Three Hundred Days of Daniel 8:14.* Battle Creek, MI: Review and Herald, 1872.

Davidson, Richard M. "The Vindication of God's Character in the Old Testament." *Journal of the Adventist Theological Society* 17, no. 1 (2006): 20–40.

Gulley, Norman R. *Systematic Theology, Vol. 3: Creation, Christ, Salvation.* Berrien Springs, MI: Andrews University Press, 2011.

Knight, George R. *The Cosmic Conflict: Understanding the Great Controversy Theme.* Hagerstown, MD: Review and Herald, 2018.

Moskala, Jiří. "Toward a Theology of God's Judgment: A Vindication of the Divine Character." *Andrews University Seminary Studies* 46, no. 2 (2008): 209–231.

Rodriguez, Ángel Manuel. *Spanning the Abyss: How the Atonement Brings God and Humanity Together.* Silver Spring, MD: Biblical Research Institute, 2008.

Waggoner, E. J. *Christ and His Righteousness*. Oakland, CA: Pacific Press, 1890.

White, Ellen G. *The Great Controversy*. Mountain View, CA: Pacific Press, 1911.

White, Ellen G. *Patriarchs and Prophets*. Mountain View, CA: Pacific Press, 1890.

White, Ellen G. *The Desire of Ages*. Mountain View, CA: Pacific Press, 1898.

White, Ellen G. *Education*. Mountain View, CA: Pacific Press, 1903.

White, Ellen G. *Christ's Object Lessons*. Washington, D.C.: Review and Herald, 1900.

White, Ellen G. *Steps to Christ*. Washington, D.C.: Review and Herald, 1892.

Supplementary and Historical Sources

Andrews University Digital Commons. *Journal of the Adventist Theological Society* and *Andrews University Seminary Studies*. Accessed 2024–2025.

Adventist Archives and Ellen G. White Estate Online Collections. Accessed 2024–2025.

Davidson, Richard M. "The Sanctuary Typology and the Vindication of God." *Adventist Theological Society Bulletin* 19 (2014): 33–47.

Knight, George R. *Turn Your Eyes Upon Jesus: Understanding the Great Controversy Theme*. Hagerstown, MD: Review and Herald, 2010.

Moskala, Jiří. "The Good News of Judgment." *Ministry Magazine* (October 2013): 10–13.

Uriah Smith. *Daniel and the Revelation*. Battle Creek, MI: Review and Herald, 1897.

James White. *Gospel Order.* Review and Herald, 1854.

J. N. Andrews. *History of the Sabbath and the First Day of the Week.* Battle Creek, MI: Steam Press, 1873.

Ángel Rodríguez. *The Sanctuary and the Atonement: Biblical, Historical, and Theological Studies.* Silver Spring, MD: Biblical Research Institute, 1981.

Whidden, Woodrow W., Jerry Moon, and John W. Reeve. *The Trinity: Understanding God's Love, His Plan of Salvation, and Christian Relationships.* Hagerstown, MD: Review and Herald, 2002.

SCRIPTURE INDEX

This section will list all Scripture references cited throughout the book in order of appearance, arranged by biblical book.

Old Testament

Genesis – 3:1–5

Job – 1:9–11

Psalms – 85:10; 145:17

Ecclesiastes – 12:13–14

Isaiah – 14:12–14; 14:13–14; 53:4–6; 53:5

Ezekiel – 28; 28:15; 28:17

Daniel – 7:10

New Testament

John – 3:16; 5:22; 5:27

Acts – 17:31

Romans – 5; 8:1–4; 11:33

Philippians – 2:13–15; 2:14–15

Hebrews – 10:16

Titus – 2:11–12

Revelation – 12:7–9; 12:10